Amazing Inventions

Inventing Cars

by Allan Morey

FOCUS READERS

BEACON

www.focusreaders.com

Focus Readers is distributed by North Star Editions:
sales@northstareditions.com | 888-417-0195

Produced for Focus Readers by Red Line Editorial.

Photographs ©: Shutterstock Images, cover, 1, 6, 8, 11, 13, 14, 17, 19, 20–21, 22, 25, 26, 29; iStockphoto, 4

Library of Congress Cataloging-in-Publication Data
Names: Morey, Allan, author.
Title: Inventing cars / by Allan Morey.
Description: Lake Elmo, MN : Focus Readers, [2022] | Series: Amazing inventions | Includes index. | Audience: Grades 2-3
Identifiers: LCCN 2021041724 (print) | LCCN 2021041725 (ebook) | ISBN 9781637390443 (hardcover) | ISBN 9781637390986 (paperback) | ISBN 9781637391525 (ebook) | ISBN 9781637392034 (pdf)
Subjects: LCSH: Automobiles--Juvenile literature. | Automobiles--History--Juvenile literature.
Classification: LCC TL147 .M65 2022 (print) | LCC TL147 (ebook) | DDC 629.222--dc23
LC record available at https://lccn.loc.gov/2021041724
LC ebook record available at https://lccn.loc.gov/2021041725

Printed in the United States of America
Mankato, MN
012022

About the Author

Allan Morey grew up on a farm in central Wisconsin. Some of his first stories were about the animals that lived on the farm. Allan now lives in Minnesota with his wife, dogs, and cats.

Table of Contents

Chapter 1

An Emergency

Lights flash. A siren wails. A police car speeds down the road. A car has crashed. The driver has been badly hurt.

The police car stops near the accident. An officer leaps out.

 A police car's flashing lights tell other drivers to move out of the way.

 Ambulances use lights and sirens when driving quickly down roads.

She grabs a first aid kit from her car's trunk. Then she rushes over to the driver. She helps him until an ambulance arrives.

EMTs put the man on a stretcher. They lift him into the back of the ambulance. Then the ambulance drives away. It races him to a hospital. The ambulance passes vans, buses, and trucks. All these vehicles carry people through the city's streets.

Did You Know?

In the United States, the first motorized police vehicle was used in 1899. It was an electric-powered wagon.

Chapter 2

The History of Cars

Inventors built the first motorized vehicles in the late 1700s. Some of these early cars got power from steam or electricity. But their engines weren't very powerful. They couldn't go very fast or far.

 Karl Benz built the first motor vehicle that used a gasoline engine. He called it the Motorwagen.

In 1886, Karl Benz built a gasoline-powered car. It could go 10 miles per hour (16 km/h). Soon, other gasoline-powered cars reached much higher speeds.

At first, cars were too expensive for most people to buy. Henry Ford changed that. He built cars using an assembly line. As a car moved down the line, workers added parts to it.

Did You Know?

Karl Benz's car had only three wheels.

 The Model T was one of Henry Ford's most popular cars.

This process made building cars faster and easier. The cars cost less, too. More people could buy them.

By the mid-1900s, millions of cars filled roads around the world.

More cars and faster speeds made driving more dangerous. So, people added safety features. After the 1960s, all cars were made with seat belts. By the late 1990s, all new cars had **airbags** as well.

People continued to improve cars and their engines. Today, some of the fastest cars can go more than 250 miles per hour (400 km/h). Some newer cars have electric

> **People plug electric cars into charging stations. Power is stored for the car to use later.**

motors. Early electric cars could travel only a few miles at a time. Then they needed to be recharged. Modern electric cars can go about 250 miles (400 km) on one charge.

Chapter 3

How Cars Work

Cars must produce power to move. Many cars have internal combustion engines. These engines use gasoline as fuel. The fuel goes into a cylinder. This is a small metal tube inside the engine.

 An internal combustion engine burns fuel to create power.

There, fuel is pressed and mixed with air. Then a spark plug **ignites** it. The fuel explodes. It pushes a piston down. This piston moves back up to push **exhaust** out of the cylinder. Then more fuel enters, and the cycle repeats.

As the pistons move up and down, they turn the car's crankshaft. The crankshaft connects to the **drivetrain**. The drivetrain makes the car's wheels turn. The car's **transmission** controls how much

Internal Combustion Engine

An internal combustion engine uses four steps, called strokes, to produce power from fuel.

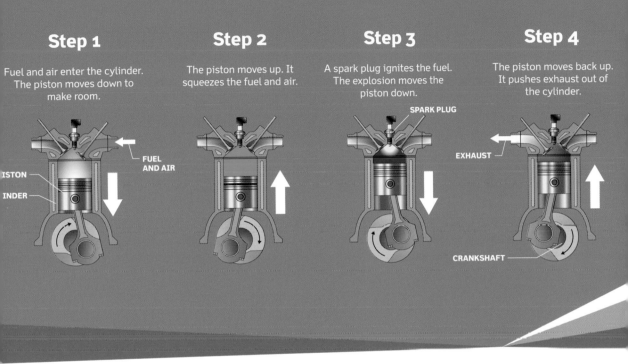

Step 1

Fuel and air enter the cylinder. The piston moves down to make room.

Step 2

The piston moves up. It squeezes the fuel and air.

Step 3

A spark plug ignites the fuel. The explosion moves the piston down.

Step 4

The piston moves back up. It pushes exhaust out of the cylinder.

SPARK PLUG

FUEL AND AIR

ISTON

INDER

EXHAUST

CRANKSHAFT

power goes to the wheels. When a driver steps on the gas pedal, more power goes to the wheels. As a result, the car speeds up.

Cars with electric motors don't have pistons, crankshafts, or transmissions. Instead, they get power from batteries. The batteries store electricity. The motor uses this energy to make the car's wheels turn.

A car's brakes and steering system are also important. When

Did You Know?

A hybrid car uses both a gasoline engine and an electric motor.

Some parking lots have spots where people can charge electric cars. People can also use outlets at their homes.

a driver presses the brake pedal, disks and pads squeeze together on the car's wheels. They slow the wheels' spinning. Drivers use the steering wheel to turn the car's front wheels.

Self-Driving Cars

As early as the 1930s, people experimented with self-driving cars. Some driverless cars were guided by magnets on the ground. But these cars weren't practical. Adding magnets to roads would be too hard and expensive.

Modern self-driving cars use computers and **sensors**. Sensors show what's around the car. The computer uses this information to steer. It plans where the car should drive. And it avoids hitting things. However, this system isn't perfect. For example, many sensors don't work in rain or snow. Scientists keep working on improvements.

Waymo is a company that makes self-driving taxis.

Chapter 4

Impacts of Cars

Cars made it easier for people to get around. Without cars, many people spent a lot of time getting to and from work. Cars let people drive right to and from places. So, they could live farther from work.

 Before cars, people often walked or used horses.

As more people used cars, countries built more roads and highways. These roads connected cities and states together. People could more easily travel to visit friends and family. Trucks could use the roads to haul cargo. People could buy things from farther away.

Did You Know?

In the 1950s, many people began moving away from cities. **Suburbs** developed.

In the United States, the Interstate Highway System includes more than 40,000 miles (64,000 km) of roads.

However, cars have negative impacts, too. Gasoline-powered cars create a lot of pollution. Their exhaust can make people sick. It's also a main cause of **climate change**.

 In large cities, air can get so polluted that it's dangerous for people to breathe.

New technologies are helping to solve these problems. Many focus on using less fuel. Electric cars are one example. Electric motors don't release exhaust. As a result, they can help create less pollution.

Electric motors still take energy to produce. This process can cause pollution. But instead of using up fuel, the motors can be charged again and again. Changes like these help people protect the environment. By using less fuel, they can do less harm to Earth.

Did You Know?

Some car engines use biofuels. These fuels are made from plants. They cause less pollution than gasoline.

FOCUS ON
Inventing Cars

Write your answers on a separate piece of paper.

1. Write a sentence describing one way that cars have changed people's lives.

2. Would you want to ride in a self-driving car? Why or why not?

3. Which part of a car is turned by moving pistons?
    A. the crankshaft
    B. the spark plug
    C. the cylinder

4. What would happen if a car's drivetrain stopped working?
    A. The car's engine wouldn't burn fuel.
    B. The car's wheels wouldn't turn.
    C. The car's brakes would fall off.

5. What does **practical** mean in this book?

*But these cars weren't **practical**. Adding magnets to roads would be too hard and expensive.*

    A. hard for most people to see
    B. easy for many people to use
    C. just part of a dream

6. What does **negative** mean in this book?

*However, cars have **negative** impacts, too. Gasoline-powered cars create a lot of pollution.*

    A. less than zero
    B. bad or harmful
    C. good or helpful

Answer key on page 32.

Glossary

airbags
Bags that pop out and fill quickly with air during a car crash to keep passengers safe.

climate change
A human-caused global crisis involving long-term changes in Earth's temperature and weather patterns.

drivetrain
The group of parts in a car that sends power to the wheels.

EMTs
People who are trained to give medical care during an emergency.

exhaust
Used gas or vapor that comes out of an engine.

ignites
Starts on fire.

sensors
Devices that collect and report information.

suburbs
Areas that are located near the edge of a larger city.

transmission
A set of gears that send power from the car's engine to the wheels.

To Learn More

BOOKS

Chandler, Matt. *The Tech Behind Electric Cars*. North Mankato, MN: Capstone Press, 2020.

Grack, Rachel. *Automobiles from Then to Now*. Mankato, MN: Amicus, 2020.

Rebman, Nick. *Earth-Friendly Transportation*. Lake Elmo, MN: Focus Readers, 2022.

NOTE TO EDUCATORS

Visit **www.focusreaders.com** to find lesson plans, activities, links, and other resources related to this title.

Index

B
batteries, 18
Benz, Karl, 10
brakes, 18–19

C
crankshafts, 16–18

D
drivetrain, 16

E
electric cars, 7, 9, 12–13,
    18, 26–27
engines, 9, 12, 15,
    17–18, 27
exhaust, 16–17, 25–26

F
Ford, Henry, 10
fuel, 15–17, 26–27

G
gasoline, 10, 15, 18,
    25, 27

H
hybrid car, 18

P
pistons, 16–18
pollution, 25–27

S
safety, 12
self-driving cars, 20

T
transmissions, 16, 18